REINFORCEMENT THEORY FOR TEACHERS

A Programed Book

Madeline Hunter, Ed.D
Principal, University Elementary School
Lecturer, Graduate School of Education
University of California, Los Angeles
Educational Consultant

TIP PUBLICATIONS
El Segundo, California

THEORY INTO PRACTICE PUBLICATIONS

Motivation Theory for Teachers
Reinforcement Theory for Teachers
Retention Theory for Teachers
Teach More—Faster!
Teach for Transfer

Additional Publications

Aide-ing in Education
Prescription For Improved Instruction

Copyright,© 1967, by Madeline Hunter
TIP Publications P.O. Box 514
El Segundo, California 90245

First Printing, June, 1967
Second Printing, September, 1968
Third Printing, September, 1969
Fourth Printing, August, 1970
Fifth Printing, February, 1971
Sixth Printing, May, 1972
Seventh Printing, April, 1973
Eighth Printing, November, 1973
Ninth Printing, May, 1975
Tenth Printing, February, 1976
Eleventh Printing, September, 1976
Twelfth Printing, March, 1977
Thirteenth Printing, August, 1977

PRINTED IN THE UNITED STATES OF AMERICA

FOREWORD

Psychological knowledge that will result in significantly increased learning of students is now available for teachers. It most cases, however, this knowledge remains unused because it is written in language that takes an advanced statistician to decode, or is buried in research journals in university libraries.

This book is one of a series written to make this important knowledge available to the classroom teacher. As such it makes no attempt to achieve comprehensive coverage of the subject, but endeavors to interpret that knowledge which is most useful in the daily decisions of teachers. The purist in learning theory may complain that some generalizations are over-simplified. Our answer would be that understanding a theory in simple form is necessary to the desire to search for increasing ramifications and complexities. The reader must also be warned that decisions based on learning theory are decisions of HOW to teach. These decisions can be made only AFTER the teacher has made decisions of WHAT content to teach and WHICH objectives are appropriate for the learner in that content area.

In other words, once a teacher has identified an appropriate educational destination for the learner, knowledge of learning theory will reveal the most effective, efficient and economical route to reach that destination.

Appreciation is expressed to the professors who made psychological theory meaningful to me when I was a student, to Dr. May Seagoe who encouraged me with her belief that it is important for all teachers, to Mrs. Margaret Devers and Mrs. Elsa Gilbert whose ability to decode my writing made a manuscript possible, and to the many teachers I have trained who continually reaffirmed my belief that there is nothing more practical than a valid theory.

Madeline Hunter

To my family who survived it, this
book is affectionately dedicated

REINFORCEMENT THEORY FOR TEACHERS

When *reinforcement theory* is mentioned a teacher conjures up visions of a Skinnerian laboratory with rats pressing bars or pigeons pecking. "Children aren't rats" is the common way of dismissing all "that laboratory nonsense" from the procedure of the classroom.

Those same teachers, when questioned about problems of the teaching profession will list children's behavior as their number one frustration. As they go on to describe this behavior, "they don't come in quietly", "I can't get their attention", "the only way Joe solves a problem is by fighting", "Susie won't even try in math", the sophisticated listener recognizes behavior that a little reinforcement "know how" could go a long way towards solving.

We have no intention of arguing here the virtues of the different theories of learning nor building understanding in depth of any one theory. It is our purpose to develop four major concepts of reinforcement which should be of value to anyone engaged in the process of learning which is essentially the process of changing behavior.

The first concept with which we must deal is positive reinforcement. *A positive reinforcer can be anything that is desired or needed by the student. A positive reinforcer will strengthen the response it follows and make that response more likely to reoccur.* This interaction between the response and the reinforcer is positive reinforcement.

Now "stimulus" and "response" may be words to which the reader has been negatively conditioned (no doubt by a poorly taught psychology course that dealt with Pavlov's salivating dogs). Consequently, for the purposes of our discussion we will substitute a child's behavior for the word "response" and what happens after his behavior, which is usually what the teacher does, as the reinforcer which produces "positive reinforcement". Thus when Johnny, working diligently, hands in his math paper and the teacher says, "Good for you!" handing in the paper is the response and "good for you" is the positive reinforcer. Saying "good for you" when Johnny hands in his math paper will make him more apt to do it again.

1

Stated in psychological terms, when a positive reinforcer ("good for you") *immediately* follows a response (handing in the math paper) it strengthens that response and increases the probability of reoccurrence of that response (Johnny will be more likely to hand in his paper next time to get more praise). The positive reinforcer must follow *immediately* to result in positive reinforcement. Saying "good for you" after a lapse in time will not accomplish much.

To simplify our discussion we will use "positive reinforcement" to indicate that a response has been followed immediately by a positive reinforcer. Let's see how much you have learned so far.

1. **We use positive reinforcement because:**

    a. It will make the child more comfortable......Turn to page 3
    (top)
    b. The teacher becomes a pleasant person......Turn to page 3
    (bottom)
    c. It will strength the response it follows........Turn to page 4
    (top)
    d. A positive approach is always better.........Turn to page 4
    (bottom)

1-a. You said we use positive reinforcement because it will make the child more comfortable.

It usually does that, but so would giving him candy or doughnuts or leaving him alone and not expecting learning. There is a more important reason for using positive reinforcement. Go back to the question on page 2 and select

1-b. You said we use positive reinforcement because the teacher becomes a pleasant person.

It may do that or she may blow her top in frustration because she has to act like things are going well even if they are not. There is a more important reason for using positive reinforcement. Go back to the question on page 2 and select the reason you think is more important.

1-c. You said we use positive reinforcement because it will strengthen the response it follows.

> GOOD FOR YOU! (Positive reinforcement. We want to strengthen your response of making correct choices.) While there are all sorts of wholesome side effects, the reason we use positive reinforcement is that we want to increase the likelihood of the response reoccurring. We want the child to "do it again".
>
> Now turn to page 5.

1-d. You said we use positive reinforcement because a positive approach is always better.

> Usually it is, but not always. You will learn why as you read further in this program. There is a more important reason for using positive reinforcement. Go back to the question on page 2 and select the reason you think is more important.

Now we come to the part that is relevant to teaching. Whenever children behave in a way that we want them to continue, *immediate* positive reinforcement will increase the likelihood that they will keep on doing it. Most of us would agree with that statement, yet our daily teaching behavior does not follow it. We usually operate on the assumption that behaving correctly is only what children should be doing, so we ignore it. Instead of doing something (positive reinforcement) so children will keep on behaving well, we only do something about it when they behave in a way they should *not* be behaving.

Let's look at an example that is all too typical. Bill comes into the classroom boisterously, obviously with no intention of settling down to the spelling task. We do something! The next day he again comes in inappropriately. We do something again! On the third day, when he comes shouting into the room, our patience has ended and WE DO SOMETHING! Bill is convinced we mean business so on the fourth day he comes in meekly and settles down to avoid the "SOMETHING". Thank goodness, we think to ourselves and proceed to the spelling lesson. The next day Bill has reverted to his old behavior. Why shouldn't he? When he acted appropriately (came in quietly) we did absolutely nothing to increase the likelihood that he would continue to act that way so his old habits took over.

2. We've all had the experience of a certain child always blurting out the answer thereby spoiling the lesson for everyone else (and our disposition for us). We insist that he raise his hand. He does and we figure it's about time. Because he has already taken so many other people's turns and blurted out so many answers we don't call on him but call on someone else. Now that we have him quiet we feel it's only fair to give someone else a turn. On our next question he again blurts out the answer. This is probably because:

a. He has had the habit so long it will take time
   to get over it .... Turn to page 6 (top)
b. He has never learned to take turns.. Turn to page 6 (bottom)
c. We did not reinforce the behavior
   we wished to reoccur............... Turn to page 7 (top)
d. He is mad because we did not
   call on him.................... Turn to page 7 (bottom)

2-a. You said he had the habit so long it will take time to get over it.

No doubt it will take a long time; however, he will never get over it if when he tries a new behavior it does not turn out well for him. Suppose you tried a new recipe and it was a fizzle. You would not keep on using it, would you? Turn back to the question on page 5 and apply what you have read about changing behavior.

2-b. You said he has never learned to take turns.

You are a good detective but this does not help you know what to do about the situation. As a teacher your deduction must shed some light on the kind of action that might solve the problem. Turn back to the question on page 5 and apply what you have read about changing behavior.

2-c. You said we did not reinforce the behavior we wish to reoccur.

EXCELLENT! (Positive reinforcement.) If a child is anxious to speak and gets to do it when he blurts out and not when he raises his hand, what do you expect? We need to call on him the first time he raises his hand to be sure he will repeat an action that works for him. Obviously we cannot continue to call on him every time he raises his hand from now on, but we will find out how to deal with that problem in a few minutes.

Now turn to page 8.

2-d. You said he is mad because we did not call on him.

No doubt. But we're mad too because we have had to put up with his behavior for a long time and this is the first time it has happened to him. Nevertheless he tried raising his hand when he wanted to speak and it got him nowhere. Turn back to the question on page 5 and apply what you have read about changing behavior.

Why didn't the "SOMETHING" that happened to boisterous Bill do the trick, you ask? That "SOMETHING" was a negative reinforcer. This brings us to our second basic principle.

A *negative reinforcer can be anything unpleasant or not desired by the student. A negative reinforcer weakens the response it immediately follows.* This can happen in two ways: 1) Negative reinforcement strengthens the response that takes away the negative reinforcer. (Bill's coming into the room quietly took away the "SOMETHING".) 2) Negative reinforcement suppresses the behavior that brought on the negative reinforcer. (The "SOMETHING" suppressed Bill's noisy entrance.)

Let us look at this principle in more homely terms. Suppose you have a pair of tan shoes that are too tight. When you wear them they hurt (negative reinforcement). So the minute you put them on you want to take them off. Taking them off (the response that takes away the hurting) is strengthened. Negative reinforcement (hurting) strengthens the response that takes it away (taking off the shoes).

Whenever you wear your tan suit you look at those shoes but you're loathe to put them on. Putting them on (the behavior that brings on the hurt) is suppressed. Negative reinforcement (hurting) suppresses the behavior that brought it on (wearing the shoes).

The hurting stops you from wearing the tan shoes with the tan suit but what shoes should you wear? The reddish brown? Or the black ones? The negative reinforcement of the hurt has given you absolutely no information about what you *should* do. You know only what you should *not* do. So you wear your black shoes. They are comfortable and you get through the day with physical ease but some mental anguish because the black shoes and the tan suit may not look well together. The next time you wear the tan suit you try the reddish brown shoes which are equally comfortable.

"What good looking shoes!" "Are they cordovan?" "They look awfully expensive." "They really look good with that suit" are the expressions you hear throughout the day. So what will you do the next time you put on that suit? Pretty obvious, isn't it?

Negative reinforcement identified what *not* to do (wear the tight shoes) but it did not tell you what *to* do. Assuming the other shoes were equally comfortable you probably would have taken turns with them until the compliments (positive reinforcement) strengthened one of your responses and made it more likely to reoccur. Notice the words "more likely". The reinforced response is not guaranteed. (You may decide to try the black shoes again or buy a new pair of tan

8

ones.) The reinforced behavior is simply more probable. (Most of the time you will choose the reddish brown ones.)

Let us look at an example of negative reinforcement in the classroom. Susie often whispers to her neighbor while you are giving instructions to the class. As a result she is uninformed and you are irritated. You decide to negatively reinforce this whispering behavior by stopping in the middle of a sentence and looking at her whenever you see her whisper. The unexpected silence causes the whole class to focus on what stopped your instruction (Susie's whispering). Your silence and all eyes on her are uncomfortable to Susie (negative reinforcement). She stops whispering and starts listening so you resume your instruction. Your immediate negative reinforcement (silence and look) has weakened Susie's response (whispering) in two ways: 1) It strengthened the response (her listening) that took it away (you stop looking and start talking). 2) It suppressed the behavior that brought it on (Susie doesn't whisper because you will give her the "silent look"). Negative reinforcement weakens the response it follows by: 1) strengthening the response that takes away the negative reinforcer and 2) suppressing the response that brings on the negative reinforcer.

It is important to remember that negative reinforcement can be dangerous. It is like a sharp knife. In the hands of a bumble-fingers, someone can get hurt. In the hands of a surgeon a sharp knife can save a life. The difference is your training and skill in the use of it.

3. When a student has been playing during his work-time most of us have tried the technique of keeping him after school to finish his work. To most children this is punishment (negative reinforcer). Which behavior do we wish to suppress by negative reinforcement?

a. Not taking his work seriously.........Turn to page 10 (top)
b. Playing during work time.........Turn to page 10 (bottom)
c. Poor work habits....................Turn to page 11 (top)
d. Not minding the teacher..........Turn to page 11 (bottom)

3-a. You said we wanted to suppress his not taking his work seriously.

Of course we would like him to think the work is meaningful and important but unfortunately not all school work is. If he were so serious he went over each problem five times, he probably would not finish and he would still need to stay after school. Go back to the question on page 9 and look for the *specific* behavior we want to suppress.

3-b. You said we wanted to suppress his playing during work time.

Right you are! And about time we did something about it. As long as he plays he will never be able to devote his full energies to the task at hand so the sooner we suppress this behavior the better. This is not to say that playing isn't normal and to be expected but society (and his future boss) won't accept playing when he should be working.
Now turn to page 12.

3-c. You said we wanted to suppress his poor work habits.

He has poor work habits all right but this is a pervasive trait and our negative reinforcer will suppress a specific behavior. We cannot hope to redesign his whole outlook on life with such a specific punishment as keeping him after school. Go back to the question on page 9 and look for the specific behavior we want to suppress.

3-d. You said we wanted to suppress his not minding the teacher.

It sounds like a desirable goal but what if some teacher uses poor judgment in giving orders. Should he mind then? Besides, we don't know that she said, "Now work and don't play." Maybe if you asked him what the teacher said he would look at you blankly because he had not even thought about it—he was just enjoying himself. Go back to the question on page 9 and look for the *specific* behavior we want to suppress.

4. Now that we have established that the negative reinforcer of keeping a boy after school will suppress his playing during work time, what response are we strengthening? Negative reinforcement is suppose to strengthen the response that takes away the negative reinforcer (staying after school). (Remember taking off the shoes that hurt?) What will take away this negative reinforcer and thereby be the response that is strengthened?

a. Finishing his work..................Turn to page 13 (top)
b. Paying attention.................Turn to page 13 (bottom)
c. Taking his work seriously...........Turn to page 14 (top)
d. Having his mother write a note that he is not
    to be kept after school.........Turn to page 14 (bottom)

4-a. You said that the response of finishing his work would be strengthened.

Now you are catching on! The minute he finishes, he's excused to go home and his staying after school is terminated. That is unless his teacher feels compelled to give him a moral lecture. If she does she has probably lost the ground gained by negative reinforcement. If she excuses him the minute he is finished he should learn that by doing what he is supposed to do he will not have to stay after school. Turn to page 15.

4-b. You said his response of paying attention would be strengthened.

Don't we wish it! But it is not that easy. Suppose he listened as hard as he could but just did not get it. He would not be able to do the work and finish. Besides, if he is a whiz in math, he would not have to listen at all, and he could figure it out and get done in time. Maddening, isn't it? You had better turn back to the question on page 12 and choose an answer that is more likely to happen.

4-c. You said taking his work seriously would be strengthened.

Could be, but we cannot count on it. Plodding Jim, who works like a dog may not finish, but Flashy Freddy can whip it out in a few minutes. Think about what behavior took away the negative reinforcer of staying after school; turn back to the question on page 12 and make another choice.

4-d. You said the response of having his mother write a note that he is *not* to be kept after school would be strengthened.

Not if he is in my school and I hope not in yours! If you choose this you must have been pushed around by parents, so quickly turn back to the question on page 12 and make another choice.

Remember negative reinforcement strengthens the response that takes away the negative reinforcer. Consequently, when cheating takes away poor grades, when day-dreaming takes away attending to work, when "telling a story" takes away consequences, all of these undesirable responses are being strengthened. This is one of the dangers of negative reinforcement. We must identify desirable behavior to replace the undesirable behavior. Then we must elicit the desirable behavior and consciously and systematically positively reinforce it. This is the only way we can be sure that some unproductive behavior (cheating, falsifying, withdrawing) which takes away the negative reinforcer is not inadvertently being reinforced.

5. We now have a boy who by negative reinforcement (staying after school) had his behavior of playing during work time suppressed (we hope) and his behavior of finishing his work strengthened (it took away the negative reinforcer of staying after school). What can we do to increase the probability that he will be more likely to use the response of finishing his work the next time that we give an assignment? (If he had been smart enough to throw up, we would have let him go home too, wouldn't we, but we don't want *that* to happen again.) Think about what you have learned to do to increase the probability of a response reoccurring.

a. Point out to him the importance of
   finishing work....................Turn to page 16 (top)
b. Calculate the amount of playtime
   he has missed.................Turn to page 16 (bottom)
c. Show him how much of our
   time he has taken.................Turn to page 17 (top)
d. Praise him for finishing his work....Turn to page 17 (bottom)

5-a. You said we would point out to him the importance of finishing his work.

> How many thousand times do you think this has happened to a child who does not finish? Obviously it was a useless technique or he wouldn't still be having the problem. He has probably learned long ago to turn off his hearing aid when adults start to lecture. Go back to the question on page 15 and select an answer that he will be sure to listen to.

5-b. You said we should calculate the amount of playtime he has missed.

> This might give him some arithmetic practice but we doubt it. Knowing the answer will probably confirm his suspicion that school takes too much time out of the more important aspects of the day and he had better sandwich more play periods into the school schedule. Go back to the question on page 15 and select an answer that will increase his desire to work.

5-c. You said to show him how much of our time he has taken.

> Depending on what kind of a fiend he is, he may shout for joy. After all, aren't we taking his time with our silly assignments? If he is truly sorry, all we have done is make him feel guilty which will in no way help him attend to his assignments. Go back to the question on page 15 and select an answer that will increase his desire to work.

5-d. You said we should praise him for finishing his work.

> Excellent! You have learned to use positive reinforcement to increase the probability of a response. If we say, "My, that's a fine job, I had no idea you could do so well. I thought perhaps you were not finishing because the work was too hard", he is going to be more apt to finish his next paper and get some more praise. The tiny hint of negative reinforcement we added (the humiliation of not being able to do the work) should suppress "not finishing" and strengthen showing you he *can* do the work. Of course, we tailor what we say and do to the needs and maturity level of the child. The words we use with a five-year-old are insulting to a twelve-year-old. The theory is the same, however. All of them (and we) respond favorably to anything that makes us feel adequate and appreciated.
> You are finding that this psychological theory is really very easy for you to understand, isn't it? You are ready to turn to the next page.

17

Now let us return to Bill and his problem of learning to enter the classroom as a student rather than a tornado. The teacher's "SOMETHING" (negative reinforcer) suppressed the behavior that brought it on but when he tried different behavior, nothing happened, so he returned to his old habits. The teacher must positively reinforce his new behavior ("Bill, you really know how a sixth grader takes care of himself") so that the likelihood of his continuing the new behavior will be increased.

Nothing happening (neither positive nor negative reinforcement) simply ignoring a response tends to make the response disappear, which brings us to our third basic principle *extinction. A response is extinguished by withholding reinforcement*. Stated as a common sense axiom, we don't keep on doing something that doesn't work. If Sally has learned to fuss to get her way and the teacher ignores it, eventually she will stop fussing to get her way with that particular teacher. (This is assuming the behavior is not reinforced in some other way such as the teacher or her playmates paying attention to her, or everyone else except that teacher giving in to the fussing.)

Scolding or ridicule (negative reinforcers) may cause Sally to suppress the fussing but it will not cause the behavior to disappear. Sally has to learn there is no point in fussing because it doesn't get any results. To extinguish a response nothing must happen as a result of it, i.e., it must have no reinforcement.

6. Four-year-old Mike has just come out with his first (to our knowledge) "damn". While playing with a group in a sand box building project he has said, "The damn truck won't work." Obviously, we would like to extinguish that part of his vocabulary. What should we do?

   a. Be sure that he sees us looking horrified
      but say nothing.....................Turn to page 19 (top)
   b. Take him to one side and explain that
      this is not appropriate language..Turn to page 19 (bottom)
   c. Stop the play and give a resounding
      lecture on swearing................Turn to page 20 (top)
   d. Act as if you had not heard it......Turn to page 20 (bottom)

6-a. You said be sure that he sees us looking horrified but say nothing.

> Horrifying a teacher is one of the most fun things a little boy can do. If he can get you to react like that to such a simple situation, who knows to what heights he might ascend if he really put his mind to it? Besides, as a result of his language nothing has happened to him—just to you. We also run the risk that he thinks we are horrified with him not his behavior. The obvious conclusion is that we don't like him and that is not a nice feeling for any little boy. Go back to the question on page 18 and choose an answer that may extinguish his "damn".

6-b. You said to take him to one side and explain this is not appropriate language.

> At least you have the sensitivity not to humiliate him in front of the group. Also, some members of the group might not have heard him and you are avoiding the undesirable possibility of teaching the word to those who may not know it. Nevertheless, if this is the first time the word has appeared, you are making too much of it. By so doing you are insuring that he will remember the word. Go back to the question on page 18 and choose an answer that has greater possibility of making him forget it.

6-c. You said stop the play and give a resounding lecture on swearing.

> You will accomplish one thing for sure. Everyone in the group (whether they knew it previously or not) will learn the word "damn". They will also learn it has the power of stopping whatever is going on and putting the teacher in orbit. Do not be surprised (if you have an alert group) that you will hear "damn" again from several sources. You had better go back to the question on page 18 and choose an answer that will have the opposite effect.

6-d. You said, act as if you had not heard it.

> You are a rapid learner and a good reader because you noticed this was the *first* time this behavior had happened. When it produces no perceivable effect it is apt to be dropped. Remember, a response is extinguished by withholding the reinforcement. We usually do not continue to do things that produce no results.
>
> No one can guarantee that he won't say "damn" again. Maybe he will get a response from his playmates or he has already "gotten" it from mother or dad. In spite of this you have chosen the most appropriate action for the first time you have heard it. *Ignoring a response helps a child forget it.*
>
> If he does not forget it, we may need some negative reinforcement to suppress the response. *Negative reinforcement helps a child remember what not to do.*
>
> See the difference?
> Now turn to the next page.

We need to clarify in more detail the difference between negative reinforcement and extinction. Negative reinforcement helps a child know what not to do. If he emits a response such as hitting another child to get a swing and the teacher scolds (negative reinforcement) he knows he should not hit. The scolding suppresses the hitting, but he still does not know an appropriate way to get the swing.

If he hits another child to get a swing and the other child ignores him, that is, the other child does nothing back but he does not give up the swing, the first child learns that hitting does not secure the swing. Nothing has happened as a result of the hitting so he tries some other way of getting the swing. The hitting response has been extinguished because it was not reinforced. Now, if by hitting he gets another child to give him the swing, the hitting has been positively reinforced and he will hit again. Let us see how clear this is.

7. Bob is a bully and he threatens other children with physical harm if they do not let him be pitcher in the ball game. The children are afraid of him and let him have his way. His behavior of threatening has been:

a. Positively reinforced...............Turn to page 22 (top)
b. Negatively reinforced .... Turn to page 22 (middle)
c. Extinguished...................Turn to page 22 (bottom)

7-a. You said his threatening behavior had been positively rein-forced.

> I'll say it has! It works so well that it will probably reoccur whenever he wants to be pitcher or anything else. You understand the principle of positive reinforcement.
> Now turn to page 23.

7-b. You said his threatening behavior has been negatively rein-forced.

> Unfortunately not! We wish it had been. His being a bully worked so well he will try it again. Turn back to the question on page 21 and select an answer that shows his response of threatening will probably happen again when he wants to be pitcher.

7-c. You said his threatening behavior has been extinguished.

> We wish it had been, but this only happens when threatening gets him no place and his threat got him the pitcher's spot. Turn back to the question on page 21 and choose an answer that will explain why he will probably act the same obnoxious way next time.

8. Let us suppose that this time Bob threatens other children and as a result the teacher puts him out of the game. His threatening has been:

a. Positively reinforced................Turn to page 24 (top)
b. Negatively reinforced............Turn to page 24 (middle)
c. Extinguished...................Turn to page 24 (bottom)

8-a. You said Bob's threatening behavior had been positively reinforced.

Thank goodness you are wrong! If it had been positively reinforced it would be likely to happen again. The teacher put him out of the game so he would *not* be so likely to act that way again. Turn back to the question on page 23 and choose an answer that shows his threatening response has been suppressed.

8-b. You said that Bob's threatening behavior had been negatively reinforced.

Right you are! Being put out of the game is something he does not like so, hopefully, even though he wants to threaten other children he will refrain from it because if he does not he won't get to play at all. The negative reinforcement (putting him out of the game) has suppressed his threatening response but he still does not know what he *should* do. Turn to page 25.

8-c. You said his threatening response has been extinguished.

Unfortunately not. When the teacher is not there to put him out of the game he will probably go back to his old bullying ways. Go back to the question on page 23 and choose an answer that shows his threatening has only been suppressed by the action of the teacher.

9. Now let us suppose that Bill begins to play with other children who are too big to be scared of him. Every time he threatens to hurt them if they do not let him pitch, they just ignore him and go on with the game. If he tries to hit one of the bigger boys, he is simply brushed off. His threatening is getting him nowhere so it is being:

a. positively reinforced................Turn to page 26 (top)
b. negatively reinforced............Turn to page 26 (middle)
c. extinguished...................Turn to page 26 (bottom)

9-a. You said his threatening behavior was positively reinforced.

> Thank goodness it was not. It didn't get him the pitching position; it got him ignored. Go back to the question on page 25 and choose an answer that shows his threatening is getting neither good nor bad results.

9-b. You said his threatening was negatively reinforced.

> No, because nothing unpleasant happened. He was just ignored. Go back to the question on page 25 and choose an answer that shows there was no reinforcement of any kind.

9-c. You said his threatening behavior was extinguished.

> Right you are! Nothing was happening as a result of his threatening so there was no point in trying it again. The absence of any kind of reinforcement will probably extinguish the behavior.
> Now turn to page 27.

Let us look at an example of application of all three of these principles (positive reinforcement, negative reinforcement, and extinguishing a response) as they might apply to whining Sally. For obvious purposes we are simplifying behavior to identify principles and this in no way should be taken as a what-to-do-about-whining recipe.

Sally has learned to whine to get her way. Obviously this has worked (been positively reinforced) in the past or she would not continue to do it. Knowing this, keeps us from the error of expecting an overnight miracle to occur or hoping by just ignoring whining it will go away (be extinguished). We wish to change her behavior. Our number one problem is what behavior do we want to produce? Too often we terminate our thinking at the "stop whining" point without proceeding to the "start. . . . . ." level. Do we want her to learn to say, "Please, may I. . . . .?" Do we want her to learn to flatter people to get her way? Do we want her to hit someone so they will give in? You recoil in horror yet these are all more effective than whining to get your way.

Thinking the problem through you will probably come to the conclusion that the behavior you want to teach is two-fold: 1) learning socially acceptable ways of persuasion (politeness, making the other person feel good about himself and you); 2) learning socially acceptable ways of dealing with your disappointment when you are not successful (going along with the majority, being a good sport).

In this analysis of behavior lie the tremendous dividends from the application of theory into practice. No longer can you be fuzzy in your thinking, for you must *identify the specific behavior you wish to change and then define with exactness the new behavior the child is to learn.* Otherwise, you have no idea what it is you are going to positively reinforce.

Let us go to work on Sally. We want to suppress the whining behavior so she will have a chance to learn to say, "Please, may I," and be a good sport if that does not work.

We start by identifying with her the specific behavior to be changed, letting her know what is not acceptable and what is. Hopefully this identification comes out of her, skillfully stimulated and guided by us. (What did you do when you wanted the ball? Did you get it? Can you think of a way that might have worked? Has this happened to other people? What did they do? Did that seem to work?) *This step of identification of the behavior with the child is essential for efficient and economical use of time and energy.* There is no point in trying to sneak up on a problem or hope that a child can guess whether it is the whining or wanting to be first up to bat that is unacceptable.

If the undesirable behavior is of long standing, it may be necessary to suppress it by negative reinforcements so another behavior can be learned in its place. ("If you whine, you will have to leave the game and sit on the bench.") The minute the desired behavior is emitted it must be heavily reinforced. ("Good for you Sally, you're being such a good sport you get the ball next.") As soon as the desired behavior (being a good sport) has been reinforced ("Good for you!") enough times so it is more likely to occur than the previous whining behavior, we remove the negative reinforcer (benching) from the undesirable behavior. Then we can extinguish it by allowing it to come out unreinforced while continuing to positively reinforce the desirable behavior.

Psychological jargon translated into Sally's behavior means that as soon as she has learned to sometimes say "please" and sometimes to be a good sport, we stop benching her for whining. When she says "please" we positively reinforce her behavior. If it is appropriate, we accede to her wishes. If inappropriate, we praise or reward her for being a good sport. When she whines we ignore her (and insist that others do the same). Hopefully, the whining will drop out of her repertoire of responses (be extinguished) while politeness and sportsmanship will become more and more likely to reoccur as a result of their being reinforced.

You may not be sure of when to negatively reinforce and when to ignore (extinguish by withholding reinforcement). It will help to estimate how often the undesirable response has occurred. If it is a new response or has not happened many times, you can ignore it. Not getting results (no reinforcement) will probably cause the child to abandon it (extinction).

If the undesirable response has happened many times, you can be sure it has worked (been positively reinforced) or the child would not continue to use it. Therefore, the undesirable response must be suppressed by negative reinforcement until some desirable response has a chance to become strong enough (as a result of positive reinforcement) to take the place of the undesirable one, i.e., be more likely to occur.

It may help if we put these ideas in another context. With a child who is having problems, it is as if you had a strong runner (undesirable behavior) and a weak runner (desirable behavior) racing for a prize. The strong runner is used to winning so you hold him back (negative reinforcement) and let the weak runner win the race and get the prize (positive reinforcement). You keep on doing this until the weak runner has had so much practice his legs are getting very strong and he enjoys running for the prize. When you think he has practiced enough that he can beat the strong runner, you let go of the formerly strong runner you have been holding back (remove negative reinforcement) so they can both race. As the previously weak runner (desirable behavior) keeps on winning (positive reinforcement), the formerly strong runner (undesirable behavior) gives up (is extinguished) because he never wins anything (no reinforcement). He won't give up as long as he is held back but if he keeps on losing (no reinforcement), he will.

10. If Johnny makes a smart remark in class and you ignore it and go right on with the lesson it means you:

    a. think it just a bad habit of his. . . . . Turn to page 30 (top)
    b. think it is a relatively new
       response for him. . . . . Turn to page 30 (middle)
    c. are not sure what you should do. . . Turn to page 30 (bottom)

10-a. You said you thought it was a bad habit.

If a response is habitual, it must be getting some results, so your ignoring it would be useless. You will have to suppress it by negative reinforcement so he can learn another response in its place. Go back to page 29 and select an answer that indicates you think *ignoring* the behavior will take care of the problem.

10-b. You said you thought it was a relatively new response for him.

Then you did just the right thing! If it were new behavior, Johnny was probably trying it out to see what would happen. When he sees it produces no results, either positive or negative, he probably will abandon it. In addition, your ignoring it will set a behavior model for the rest of the class. If smart remarks do not get a big reaction from you, there will be little point in anyone else trying them.
Turn to page 31.

10-c. You said you were not sure what you should do.

If you are a teacher this is not the first nor last time you will find yourself in this fix. However, you have just negatively reinforced the writer of this program for not writing more clearly, so turn back to page 29 and re-read the material there.

11. Now let us assume that you ignore Johnny's smart (and rude) remark but it puts the rest of the class in hysterics. At this point you should decide to:

a. keep on ignoring the behavior.........Turn to page 32 (top)
b. negatively reinforce Johnny.......Turn to page 32 (middle)
c. negatively reinforce the class......Turn to page 32 (bottom)

11-a. You said you would keep on ignoring the behavior.

If you do you have more ability to tolerate misbehavior than most teachers. You will need it too, as the class sees someone can get by with unacceptable classroom manners. Turn back to the question on page 31 and select an answer that will give a boy some assistance with the self control he lacks.

11-b. You said you would negatively reinforce Johnny.

Good for you—he needs it! For his sake and yours that kind of behavior should be suppressed. What you use for a negative reinforcer depends on Johnny's personality. Whether you quietly say, "Let's plan a time when we can talk" or you suspend him from your class depends on your judgment of which is more appropriate. The wiser your decision the more effective will be the negative reinforcement. Remember that the behavior that removes your negative reinforcer will be strengthened so you had better be sure that it is desirable behavior.

Now turn to page 33.

11-c. You said you would negatively reinforce the class.

You would no doubt feel like it but Johnny is the culprit. The class is probably looking to you to control Johnny and then they will control themselves. Turn back to the question on page 31 and choose an answer that will assist Johnny in suppressing his rudeness.

One small matter remains to thwart us. We may have Sally's whining problem all nicely solved and then after Christmas vacation we find to our horror that she has returned to her whining, a behavior we have not seen since the middle of November. *Spontaneous recovery* is the term used to describe this reoccurrence of behavior you thought had been extinguished. It simply means that after a period of no appearance an old habit will "recover" enough to once more emerge. Again it needs to be "laid to rest" by withholding reinforcement (ignoring the behavior). The temptation to "blow your top" when Sally again whines must be sternly controlled so there is no reinforcement whatsoever, either postive or negative, and the whining response can be extinguished.

Now our theory is beginning to take shape in terms of what we do in the classroom. Oversimplified, we can state that we first identify the behavior we want to change and define the new behavior we wish the child to learn. Next we eliminate the behavior we don't want by either suppressing it with negative reinforcement or extinguishing it by ignoring it. We can achieve the behavior we *do* want by getting the child to behave that way and then positively reinforcing the response.

Notice that an important part of our learning strategy is to get the child to behave in a way we *do* want so we have something to reinforce. This may take all kinds of conniving on our part. We may need to meet tornado Bill at the door, hand him a load of books, and ask him to place them on the table before he sits down. The situation will be just different enough that he will probably comply. Then we step in with positive reinforcement. "Bill, you certainly know how to come into the room", or the like.

We may need to sneak up on whining Sally with "Boys and girls, watch Sally, she doesn't fuss when it's not her turn, look what a good sport she is!" There are few children who can resist the strategy of the master teacher. *Then* you have some behavior to reinforce!

It all sounds so simple, doesn't it? Then why doesn't it always work? The answer to this brings us to our final principle concerning *schedule of reinforcement* or "practice". *Schedule refers to the relationship of frequency of the behavior to the frequency of reinforcement.* We can vary this schedule by saying "good for you" (positive reinforcement) every time Johnny comes in quietly, every other time, every fifth time, or whenever we happen to be in a good mood.

Decisions regarding the schedule of reinforcement are usually made unconsciously by the teacher depending on her mood, how much the behavior irritates her, or personality factors relating to her consistency. It is unfortunate that this is so. These decisions should be made at a conscious level for they have direct bearing on the rapidity with which children learn a new response and the ease with which they forget it and return to their old behavior.

A *regular schedule of reinforcement* or reinforcing a response every time it occurs makes for fast learning. Saying "Good for you!" every time Bill comes in quietly will achieve the new behavior rapidly (all other things being equal of course). His forgetting curve will match his learning curve however, so when you stop reinforcing him his good behavior will be extinguished just as rapidly. Then, "what's the use," you say—only too often all your efforts in teaching are for naught. Here is where changing schedules comes in, so that his response will be resistant to forgetting. You now need to use an intermittent schedule of reinforcement where you do not reinforce a response every time but reinforce intermittently, for example, the first, third, sixth, and tenth in a series of ten responses. This intermittent schedule of reinforcement is what makes behavior persistent and resistant to forgetting.

Let us look at tornado Bill's behavior again. For a week now he has been coming in quietly in the morning, from recess, from noon, and from physical education. You have reinforced him every time —in fact, he now looks expectantly at you for praise. You decide you are no longer concerned with his learning the response, for this has been accomplished. The problem now becomes how long he will remember it when you are busy with other children and not around to praise him. So you decide to switch to an intermittent schedule of reinforcement (good old theory, it tells you what might be productive rather than your having to reach helplessly into a behavior grab bag).

Now you have a plan for Bill. When he comes in quietly you give him especially hearty positive reinforcement. ("Bill, you just *never* forget to be grown up.") After recess, when he comes in appropriately and looks to you for approval, you are busy putting the math assignment on the board—with the eye in back of your head watching Bill carefully. If he follows the usual pattern he will look disappointed but settle down. After lunch you will be conspiciously watching (to eliminate any possibility of his returning to his old behavior) and reward him with, "You just dont need a teacher at all. Why even when I'm busy with something else you know what to do!" That ought to hold him without additional reinforcement for the rest of the day.

The next morning you again heartily reinforce him. (Remember that old spontaneous recovery may take place overnight.) This time you might be able to wait until afternoon dismissal and terminate the day with, "Bill, you've come in perfectly all day today without my even looking at you." Hopefully before long you can pretty much forget you ever had to worry about Bill being a tornado. Occasional reinforcement will maintain the strength of his behavior and the intermittent schedule will develop resistance to forgetting.

Now let us see if you understand when to use a regular and when to use an intermittent schedule of reinforcement.

12. **If Jane is learning a new process in mathematics, you should reinforce her correct solutions:**

    a. every time........................Turn to page 36 (top)
    b. every other time.................Turn to page 36 (middle)
    c. at intermittent intervals..........Turn to page 36 (bottom)

12-a. You said you should reinforce her correct solutions every time.

You bet you should! A regular schedule of reinforcement makes for fast learning. Keep on selecting the right answers to our question and you will know the satisfaction Jane feels. Besides, you are positively reinforcing us as a writer of programs.

Now turn to page 37.

12-b. You said we should reinforce her every other time.

Not unless we are only "teaching" half of the time. We want her to learn rapidly. Go back to the question on page 35 and select an answer that will continually convince her she is really on the right track.

12-c. You said we should reinforce her at intermittent intervals.

After she has really learned the process this is a good idea. While she is learning, it will slow her down because she will not be sure she is right. Go back to the question on page 35 and choose an answer that will let her know every time she is right.

13. **Once Jane has learned the new mathematics process, you want to make sure she remembers it even when you are not there to tell her she is right. To develop resistance to forgetting you change to:**

a. a regular schedule of reinforcement...Turn to page 38 (top)
b. an intermittent schedule
   of reinforcement.................Turn to page 38 (middle)
c. some schedule related to the
   particular situation..............Turn to page 38 (bottom)

13-a. You said you would change to a regular schedule of rein-forcement.

> That would be no change at all. If you know your learning theory you have been using a regular schedule and reinforcing her every time she has made the correct response so she will learn rapidly. Turn back to the question on page 37 and choose an answer that will make her new skill resistant to forgetting.

13-b. You said you would change to an intermittent schedule.

> Good for you! Once a response has been learned, when you receive a reward for it some times and not others you always have hope that the next time will be rewarded. Slot machines are built on the principle that if they pay off occasionally, people will keep putting money into them. Las Vegas exists on intermittent reinforcement. Once people enjoy gambling, just an occasional pay-off will keep them playing.
> Turn now to page 39.

13-c. You said you would change to some schedule related to the particular situation.

> We would hope your behavior would be relevant to the situation as it was described. Go back to the question on page 37, re-read the particular problem and choose the answer that will make the response resistant to extinction (forgetting).

Let us practice what we know.

Peter is a clown in class. He uses his skill to get attention, make people laugh, and break up the class at the times he desires. You are tempted to "break him up" but your professional training (thank goodness) tells you that (a) he wishes attention, (b) he has been successful in getting it by these methods, (c) he probably does not get it by other methods (or he would be using them), (d) he may be clowning as behavior to cope with situations he cannot handle in any other way, i.e., he does not know the right answer to the question you ask, or (e) because he is not popular, he does not think he will get attention from the group in any other way.

He obviously has his needs but you have yours—and an orderly controlled classroom is rightfully one of them. Letting him continue clowning may make him think he will feel more comfortable for the moment; but it is not a productive coping mechanism, and we have a responsibility for helping him develop a better one.

14.   Number one step in changing his behavior is:

a. Help him identify the behavior
   to be changed.....................Turn to page 40 (top)
b. Ignore the clowning..............Turn to page 40 (bottom)
c. Negatively reinforce
   the clowning......................Turn to page 41 (top)
d. Positively reinforce
   his good behavior.............Turn to page 41 (bottom)

14-a. You said the first step was to help him identify the behavior to be changed.

Perfect! You are on your way! He needs to have his old habit brought to a conscious level. (His typical response when you reprimand him is, "What did *I* do? I just said . . . "). But remember when you say "Stop clowning" you need to get him to decide what he should start doing. If the new response (start helping with your good ideas) is incompatible with the old response (clowning), then one has to replace the other and you have really changed behavior. It is no use working with responses that could happen together (clowning and giving right answers) because one does not have to replace the other.

This step sounds easy but it is not. The trick is to have *him* identify the problem and suggest solutions to it. Your *telling* him what he should do will just be another episode in a long series of unsuccessful attempts by well-meaning (but psychologically uninformed) people. It also helps if he can identify the frequency with which this behavior is occurring. ("Peter, were you aware that this happened six times today? Let's keep track of the number of times it happens tomorrow so we'll know how much of a habit it is.") Not only have you identified the problem but you have established a way of measuring growth in behavior. When clowning occurs only once a day you know you are on the right track. If you don't know he has reduced it from a six to one incidence, you are apt to be vulnerable to that there-he-goes again feeling. This was a long way of saying, "Your answer was absolutely right"; so turn now to page 42 for the second step in our reformation of Peter.

14-b. You said to ignore the clowning.

If this were the first time it happened, you would be absolutely right but this is behavior of long standing. Ignoring it will probably convince Peter and the class that you feel helpless about the possibility of doing anything about it. Turn back to the question on page 39 and choose an answer that will be easier on your blood pressure.

14-c. You said to negatively reinforce the clowning.

You are on the right track but you are ahead of yourself. You need to make sure that Peter is aware of what it is about his behavior that is unacceptable. If you scold it will be difficult to determine whether you are mad at him or at the class for laughing at him. If you were Peter which would you choose to think? Go back to the question on page 39 and decide the first thing you need to do.

14-d. You said to positively reinforce his good behavior.

We hope you do. But if you are a good teacher, you have been doing that right along and he is still clowning. Here is where just emphasizing the positive will not work. He is getting too much satisfaction from his negative behavior. Go back to the question on page 39 and choose an answer that will interrupt the behavior pattern he has developed.

15. After Peter has identified his problem as clowning and re-
    alizes he uses this technique far too often each day, what can
    we do next that will most effectively change his behavior? (Re-
    member, when a child has to stop doing one thing he has to
    start doing something else.)

    a. Negatively reinforce the clowning. . . . . Turn to page 43 (top)
    b. Extinguish the clowning . . . . Turn to page 43 (bottom)
    c. Positively reinforce some behavior
       incompatible with clowning . . . . Turn to page 44 (top)
    d. Ridicule him for clowning . . . . Turn to page 44 (bottom)

15-a. You said we should negatively reinforce the clowning.

That would be a good way to say "Stop clowning!" But what is he to start doing? He needs to have a desirable alternative to the response that he knows best. If the new response is something he cannot do when he clowns, you have the answer. Turn back to the question on page 42 and pick an answer that will do just that.

15-b. You said we should extinguish the clowning.

Eventually we will have to, but before we can do it he will have to develop a better response that he can use when he feels the urge to clown. Go back to the question on page 42 and choose an answer that incorporates this idea.

15-c. You said we should positively reinforce some behavior incompatible with the clowning.

Right you are! If he develops some new behavior such as giving serious answers or furthering class discussion, we can give heavy positive reinforcement and make this kind of response more probable than the clowning response. Eventually we will have to extinguish the clowning response by letting it come out reinforced, but we want to be sure his acceptable response has been reinforced enough to be more probable.

Now turn to page 45.

15-d. You said we should ridicule him for clowning.

The negative reinforcement would tend to suppress the clowning but he only knows what not to do (clown). What should he do? He has to know what the acceptable behavior is so he can practice it and we can reinforce it. Go back to the question on page 42 and choose an answer that incorporates this idea.

16. Now that Peter knows he will be rewarded with praise when he gives serious answers and furthers class discussion, in order to be sure his acceptable response is more probable, we should:

a. Plan situations where he will respond well and praise him every time he does .... Turn to page 46 (top)

b. Negatively reinforce him when he clowns. . Turn to page 46 (middle)

c. Change to an intermittent schedule of praise when he gives serious answers .... Turn to page 46 (bottom)

16-a. You said we should plan situations where he will respond well and praise him every time he does.

You are absolutely right. We want him to learn rapidly and a regular schedule of reinforcement will do it. Once he knows the behavior, we can change to an intermittent schedule so the behavior will be resistant to forgetting. By then his clowning behavior may have been extinguished. Now turn to page 47.

16-b. You said we should negatively reinforce him when he clowns.

We may not need to. We will have to see first whether or not we can teach the new response without suppressing the clowning response. Turn back to the question on page 45 and select an answer that will help him quickly learn the appropriate response.

16-c. You said we should change to an intermittent scchedule of praise when he gives serious answers.

Eventually we will need to, but he is not ready for that yet, because we are not sure his serious answers are more probable than his clowning behavior. Go back to the question on page 45 and select an answer that will make his new behavior stronger.

There, you have the four most important concepts of reinforcement—positive, negative, extinction, and schedule. Why then can't we shape behavior as easily and successfully in the classroom as we can in a psychology laboratory? Here again theory helps us understand. By the time the child arrives at our classroom door he has a long history of conditioning and reinforcement. How many thousand times has a child interrupted, whined, fought, or been a poor sport before you decided to do something about it? As we said before, it must have worked for him or he would not be continuing it. The behavior would have been extinguished.

The problem is compounded by the fact that in most cases other people have attempted to change the undesirable behavior and have given up. (Sally's mother decides she is not going to give in to whining so she resists it a few times and then capitulates.) As a result, the behavior has received reinforcement on an intermittent schedule which makes it more resistant to extinction.

If we were to write a "how-to-change-behavior" recipe, it would look something like this:

Step 1. Identify (first for yourself and then with the child) the behavior to be changed and the new behavior that is to replace the old.

Step 2. Decide what constitutes positive and negative reinforcement. Devise a strategy to get the new behavior and determine the way you will positively reinforce it.

Step 3. Decide whether the old behavior is so strong you need to suppress it by negative reinforcement or whether lack of any kind of reinforcement will extinguish it. If you decide to use negative reinforcement, determine what it will be. Remember, the student's behavior that removes your negative reinforcer, is being strengthened. So be careful!

Step 4. Develop a strategy to get the child to practice the new behavior and positively reinforce it on a regular schedule (every time).

Step 5. As soon as the child has practiced the new behavior enough so it is more likely than the old behavior, remove any negative reinforcement so the old behavior can occur with no reinforcement and be extinguished.

Step 6. Change to an intermittent schedule of reinforcing the new behavior (make the intervals between reinforcement increasingly long) so the new behavior will be resistant to forgetting.

Step 7. Know that occasionally the child will slip back into his old behavior (spontaneous recovery) but now you know how to achieve the new behavior.

17. Let us practice by trying these psychological principles on the child who is a constant talker in the classroom. (Does this remind you of one of yours?) What is the first thing we do?

a. Extinguish the response...............Turn to page 49 (top)
b. Negatively reinforce.............Turn to page 49 (bottom)
c. Positively reinforce..................Turn to page 50 (top)
d. Identify the behavior
   to be changed...................Turn to page 50 (bottom)

17-a. You said we extinguish the response.

Don't we wish it! You extinguish a response by ignoring it and the only thing that ignoring it will accomplish for us is best described by our psychiatrist. No, the talking habit is too pervasive, it will continue unless we do something. Go back to the question on page 48 and choose something the teacher can do.

17-b. You said we negatively reinforce talking.

And how! But how is the child going to know if we are blasting him for talking, not working, disturbing his neighbors, or irritating us? Go back to the question on page 48 and choose an answer that will leave no question in his mind.

17-c. You said we should positively reinforce him.

It would take a saint to overlook the fact that he is constantly running off at the mouth. We may be able to give him positive reinforcement in some areas but not for control of his vocal chords. Go back to the question on page 48 and choose an answer that will put some responsibility on him.

17-d. You said we should identify the behavior to be changed.

Absolutely correct! He needs to know what we are concerned about and why. Here again the skilled teacher gets him to think through the problem. (Don't be surprised if he really believes he should not talk because we don't like it.) Remember our technique of recording the frequency of the response (the number of times a day that he is talking when he should not). This will help him focus on the severity of the problem and establish a base line for computing growth. Now let us go to the next step of our plan for changing his behavior.

Turn to page 51.

18. Our habitual talker has identified his problem behavior and resolved to do something about it. How do we help him keep from falling right back into his old talking habit?

a. We identify it for him.............Turn to page 52 (top)
b. We negatively reinforce it........Turn to page 52 (bottom)
c. We positively reinforce it...........Turn to page 53 (top)
d. We extinguish it...............Turn to page 53 (bottom)

18-a. You said we identify it for him.

We just did, or rather he did it for himself. Now that he knows what the problem is, go back to the question on page 51 and see what we can do to help.

18-b. We negatively reinforce it.

You bet we do! We want that talking suppressed. We might signal him when he is doing it. If that does not work, we can walk over, get a piece of paper, and record it. All of this, of course, without anyone else knowing the plan. It is strictly a private matter between you and the child and nobody else's business. If we need to make our negative reinforcement stronger, we put a tally mark on the board without letting the rest of the class know why. The culprit is really going to seek a response (which is to stop talking) that will take that negative reinforcer away before the rest catch on to what you are tallying. So, you are in business. Negative reinforcement has suppressed the response (talking) that brought it on and strengthened the response (not talking) that takes it away. Neat, isn't it?

We again need to warn you that if some undesirable response, such as daydreaming, removes the negative reinforcer, that response will be strengthened. So watch out!

Now turn to page 54.

18-c. You said we positively reinforce it.

You must be kidding or else you are getting ready to re-sign and let someone else cope with him. Go back to the question on page 51 and choose an answer that will make him talk *less*.

18-d. You said we extinguish it.

Eventually we have to, but right now it is much too strong to die by itself. Doing nothing simply means we are admitting that there is nothing we can do and we are not at that point. Go back to page 51 and choose an answer that will show him who is boss.

19. We have helped our talker identify his problem behavior. We have negatively reinforced his behavior so his talking is suppressed and his not talking is strengthened. Now what can we do to be sure he spends increasing time in a not talking (and consequently listening and learning) state?

a. We switch to an intermittent schedule.. Turn to page 55 (top)
b. We extinguish his talking........ Turn to page 55 (bottom)
c. We use negative reinforcement....... Turn to page 56 (top)
d. We use positive reinforcement.... Turn to page 56 (bottom)

19-a. You said we switch to an intermittent schedule.

You are on the right track but ahead of yourself. His not-talking-listening-and-learning response is new to him and not strong enough yet to be more probable than his habitual talking response. Go back to page 54 and choose an answer that will strengthen the response you want.

19-b. You said we extinguish his talking.

It is a step we need to take but he is not ready for it yet. He is still not sure this "not talking" is really going to pay off. Go back to page 54 and choose a response that will convince him it is the way to the good life.

19-c. You said we use negative reinforcement.

We have already done this. Of course maybe you are so fed up with him you would like to do it again but now we need to move to the next step. Go back to the question on page 54 and choose an answer that will increase the behavior we want.

19-d. You said we should use positive reinforcement.

You are absolutely right! Now that we have him quiet we have to do something so he knows this is the way it should be. Excusing him first because he has worked so quietly, praising his business-like way of handling his school work, writing his mother a note telling her what a wonderful boy she has, or accusing him of never giving you an opportunity to scold him any more, all may be effective rewards depending on you, him, and the situation. Once is not enough but again, and again, and again he has to be reinforced on a regular schedule until his new behavior becomes stronger than his old talking behavior.

Now turn to page 57.

20. Now that you have a quiet worker, do you have to keep praising him the rest of his life so he won't slip back? Not if you:

a. Record his success..................Turn to page 58 (top)

b. Change to an intermittent
schedule......................Turn to page 58 (bottom)

c. Make it habitual..................Turn to page 59 (top)

d. Let him know that is
what you expect...............Turn to page 59 (bottom)

20-a. You said we should record his success.

> We hope you have already done it. That is part of his positive reinforcement and is technically known as *knowledge of results*. It will certainly tend to strengthen his response but go back to page 57 and choose an answer that will keep him from slipping back into his old habits.

20-b. You said we should change to an intermittent schedule.

> Absolutely! You remembered that once we established a response by regular reinforcement we needed to change to an intermittent schedule to make it rèsistant to forgetting. You recall we skipped reinforcing one time and then went back to it, skipped more and went back, etc. It is like a review with the intervals between practice getting longer and longer. It really works!
> Now turn to page 60.

20-c. You said we make it habitual.

That we do, but how? Go back to the question on page 57 and choose an answer that will do the trick.

20-d. You said we let him know that is what we expect.

Other teachers have tried this with him and you got the results of their labors. That should be enough to make you go back to page 57 and pick a different answer.

An important aspect of our understanding of reinforcement is that while we usually associate praise and reward with positive reinforcement and punishment with negative reinforcement, this is not necessarily so. Shy Tommy might find public praise a very embarrassing and undesirable negative reinforcer, and attention-seeking Paul might find a public scolding very rewarding to his needs (positive reinforcement). As a result, while we can make some general assumptions, it is always necessary to correct them by an estimate of what constitutes reward and punishment for a particular child. "Identifying the reward system to which he responds" is the way we say it psychologically.

The last important consideration to which we must attend, is that emotions and attitudes are responses which children cannot control; but they become associated with the actions that bring rewards and punishment. As a result, these emotions and attitudes are conditioned in a respondent fashion like Pavlov's salivating dog. We don't need to worry about our positive reinforcement, but we need to be concerned about the environment and emotions that may become conditioned by negative reinforcement. It is this aspect that makes punishment a dangerous weapon. Scolding or benching Sally may suppress her whining, but it may also teach her that teachers are mean, games are not fun, and the play yard is a place to be avoided by playing in the girls' lavatory.

21. **Knowing reinforcement theory makes you realize that corporal punishment (negative reinforcement) is not a good idea because:**

    a. It is old-fashioned.................Turn to page 61 (top)
    b. It is ineffective.................Turn to page 61 (bottom)
    c. It is too hard on the teacher........Turn to page 62 (top)
    d. Emotions and attitudes are conditioned
       by it....................... Turn to page 62 (bottom)

21-a. You said it is old-fashioned.

It is, but so are honesty and integrity. Being old-fashioned can be a virtue as well as something to be discarded. Go back to the question on page 60 and choose an answer that describes why it is not good.

21-b. You said it is ineffective.

Often it is. Nevertheless, a good spanking may stop a behavior we do not like. We agree that there are more effective ways to change behavior but go back to the question on page 60 and choose an answer that will more precisely describe the undesirable results of corporal punishment.

21-c. You said it is too hard on the teacher.

If you know anything harder than good teaching, we will put in with you. Granted, if you have ever had to spank a child it is an extremely unpleasant memory; but if it would work, it might be worth it. Go back to the question on page 60 and choose an answer that will justify your not doing it.

21-d. You said emotions and attitudes are conditioned by it.

They certainly are! A child may learn not to do a certain thing as a result of a spanking. He also will possibly learn to dislike school, that teachers are mean, rules are not fair, and to get even the first chance he has. All of these compounding factors make corporal punishment a negative reinforcer that usually is educationally unsound. There are many other consequences that are just as effective (or more so) and do not have the undesirable side effects.

Now turn to page 63.

In our discussion, we have neglected one important factor and that is the reason the undesirable behavior started in the first place. Possibly Bill is afraid he cannot succeed in school and his tornado behavior is a form of bravado that covers up his fright. Perhaps Sally's mother rejects her and whining is the way she expresses unhappiness with herself and her role in the world. Changing behavior by reinforcement in no way removes the cause. Still, whining and misbehavior are compounding factors to an already disturbed child. They do not help the situation, they make it worse, as an anxious boy and a rejected girl incur teacher and peer group disapproval. Changing that behavior does not solve the problem, but it prevents it from becoming even more unmanageable. As acceptable behavior develops, the child has the compensatory advantage of acceptance and success at school.

Now let us apply our reinforcement theory to you, a classroom teacher. We have identified the problem of using reinforcement in your teaching. We have sounded the threats (negative reinforcement) of what is apt to happen if you use punishment. So, hopefully, you will suppress the temptation to notice only that which is not right, and scold about it. We have suggested some alternate patterns of behavior for you (praise and reward) and talked glowingly of what they will do for your teaching (positive reinforcement). Being "wishy-washy" about your teaching will get you nowhere so, hopefully, that behavior will be extinguished. Because, as a human being, you are probably not as consistent as you would like to be, you will forget to reinforce part of the time so you are already on an intermittent schedule.

As you use these ideas, picture this programed book standing behind your teaching behavior saying, "Good for you. You really know how to use reinforcement theory!" (Positive reinforcement.) The real reinforcement will come as you experience the reward of children's learning. Isn't that why you are in this profession?

REINFORCEMENT THEORY
SELF TEST

If you wish to give yourself some positive (we hope) reinforcement by knowing how much you have learned, take this test.

Let us assume you have decided to train your group of boys and girls to stop whatever they are doing and look at you when you give some pre-arranged signal. (If you have not decided this with every group of students you teach, you had better start now.)

1. You will need to give the signal and:
   a. have them show others how well they can do it
   b. punish those who do not respond
   c. give them practice
   d. praise those who do it well
   e. explain it again

2. At first you will need to:
   a. praise them every time they respond well
   b. praise them every other time they respond well
   c. praise them at irregular times
   d. punish those who do not respond every time
   e. punish those who do not respond at irregular times

3. If you praise the children who look up at the signal and ignore those who do not, you are attempting to:
   a. negatively reinforce
   b. give practice
   c. switch to an intermittent schedule of reinforcement
   d. use a regular schedule of reinforcement
   e. extinguish the response of not looking up

4. If you negatively reinforce children who do not look up at the signal, it means:
   a. you want the children to know you mean business
   b. you want to identify the non-conformers
   c. you think ignoring the offenders will not make the behavior disappear
   d. children need to know the consequences of their acts
   e. you think misbehavior should be punished

5. If you punish a child who does not respond to the signal, it means you:
   a. want children to know you are aware of those who do not look at you
   b. want to suppress his "not looking at you"
   c. want to shape his behavior
   d. want to be fair to the other children who always look at you
   e. are alert to the identification of children who have not yet learned the behavior

6. If possible, you should avoid punishment because:
   a. a positive approach is always better
   b. it isn't very effective
   c. it won't extinguish a response
   d. it may have undesirable side-effects
   e. children will resent it

7. In order to be sure the children do not easily forget their response to the signal, you will need to:
   a. remind them often
   b. punish those who forget
   c. switch to an intermittent schedule where you praise them occasionally
   d. give them lots of practice
   e. use a regular schedule where you praise them every time

8. If you wish to change behavior, it is essential that you know that punishment:
    a. will not extinguish a response
    b. is a negative approach
    c. gives children a wrong impression of the teacher
    d. is sometimes necessary
    e. will not shape behavior

9. Johnny is talking and the teacher frowns at him. He stops and once again she looks pleasant. His response of not talking has been strengthened because:
    a. it took away the frown
    b. the class has noticed the teacher frowning at him
    c. the teacher may report his behavior to his mother
    d. the frown reminds him of the "no talking" rule
    e. talking got him in trouble

10. Saying "be careful when you work" is not reinforcement because:
    a. it is not positive
    b. it does not follow a response
    c. it may not be needed
    d. it is not appropriate for all children
    e. children should remember it themselves

11. When Jim picks up paper on the yard, the teacher praises him. Her praise should be:
    a. reinforcement
    b. identification of behavior
    c. positive reinforcement
    d. a regular schedule of reinforcement
    e. an intermittent schedule of reinforcement

12. The children come into the room with the teacher watching. She says they are acting very grown up when they take out their spelling books. They study quietly and get ready for their spelling test. Which behavior is the most likely to reoccur?
    a. coming in quietly
    b. taking out their spelling books
    c. study quietly
    d. get ready for the test
    e. all of these

13. Ignoring a child's undesirable behavior should indicate the teacher:
    a. feels she should not make too much of it
    b. can't pay attention to everything
    c. has not seen it
    d. wishes to extinguish the behavior
    e. feels negative reinforcement is inappropriate

14. In order for behavior to be resistant to forgetting a teacher must:
    a. positively reinforce it every time it occurs
    b. positively reinforce it every other time it occurs
    c. positively reinforce it intermittently
    d. positively reinforce differently for different problems
    e. positively reinforce differently for different children

15. When a teacher wishes a child to learn a new response as quickly as possible she should use:
    a. positive reinforcement
    b. negative reinforcement
    c. extinction
    d. a regular schedule of positive reinforcement
    e. an intermittent schedule of positive reinforcement

16. A teacher tells a student he must stop being a poor sport and she will punish him if the behavior continues. Her major error has been:
    a. using negative reinforcement
    b. not using positive reinforcement
    c. identifying the undesirable behavior
    d. not identifying the desirable behavior
    e. conditioning him against sports

17. Bob never listens to instructions. After they are given, he always asks a dozen unnecessary questions. You do not wish to discourage valid questions, but you think he should develop the ability to attend well enough so he will need to ask only about areas not covered in the instructions. As Bob begins to listen carefully to instructions, you will need to:
    a. praise him every time
    b. praise him every other time
    c. praise him at the times it seems appropriate
    d. punish children who don't listen every time
    e. occasionally punish children who do not listen

18. If you praise Bob's good questions and ignore his foolish ones, it is because you:
    a. are accentuating the positive
    b. believe that by praising the good ones, the poor ones will disappear
    c. don't wish to humiliate him in front of the group
    d. it sets an example for others
    e. wish him to build self confidence

19. You have decided to praise Bob for asking good questions because:
    a. it shows he is really thinking
    b. he had to hear the instructions in order to frame a good question
    c. it's important that children feel free to ask questions
    d. it sets an example for others
    e. he needs to know you are not picking on him

20. After Bob has learned to listen well and you praise him only occasionally for listening and following directions you are:
    a. making sure the other children don't feel slighted
    b. being a normal human being who does not always remember
    c. feeling he should be able to go on his own
    d. making sure his listening will continue even if you are not the teacher
    e. ready to move on to his next learning task

Correct answers

1—d	6—d	11—c	16—d
2—a	7—c	12—b	17—a
3—e	8—a	13—d	18—b
4—c	9—a	14—c	19—b
5—b	10—b	15—d	20—d

If you have more than 15 correct—

You're a whiz! (positive reinforcement)

If you have 7–14 correct—

You're doing okay, but you may need to review parts of this book so you will increase your success in the classroom.

If you have less than 7 correct—

Shame on us! (negative reinforcement)   Turn back to page one and if you still don't get it, write us a letter so we can revise this book.